The author used many research documents, books, and websites to gather the information for this book. Where possible, we've used the most up-to-date statistics, and in places, the author has used averages or amalgamated data. To help with understanding, many of the figures given are approximate, and where only a fraction of a person would have appeared, it has been rounded up. Every effort has been made to ensure the accuracy of the information in the first edition of this book, published in 2021.

Here is a list of sources used for this book:

British Council
britishcouncil.org/research-policy-insight/policy-reports/the-english-effect [pp. 2 and 5]

The Brookings Institution
brookings.edu/blog/future-development/2020/10/22/are-we-on-track-to-end-global-hunger/

Central Intelligence Agency
cia.gov/the-world-factbook/

European Commission: Global Human Settlement
ghsl.jrc.ec.europa.eu/atlasOverview.php

The Global Education Project
theglobaleducationproject.org/earth/human-conditions.php#2

The Guardian/**Oxfam**
theguardian.com/business/2019/jan/21/world-26-richest-people-own-as-much-as-poorest-50-per-cent-oxfam-report

International Energy Agency
iea.org/reports/sdg7-data-and-projections/access-to-electricity

National Bureau of Economic Research
A New Data Set of Educational Attainment in the World, 1950–2010
Robert J. Barro and Jong-Wha Lee
nber.org/papers/w15902

National Human Genome Research Institute
genome.gov/about-genomics/fact-sheets/Genetics-vs-Genomics

Our World in Data (University of Oxford)
ourworldindata.org/energy
ourworldindata.org/energy-access
ourworldindata.org/global-education
Global Education, 2020, Max Roser and Esteban Ortiz-Ospina
ourworldindata.org/homelessness
ourworldindata.org/literacy
ourworldindata.org/urbanization
ourworldindata.org/world-population-growth

Share the World's Resources (STWR)
sharing.org/information-centre/reports/estimated-100-million-people-are-homeless-worldwide

Statista
statista.com/statistics/266808/the-most-spoken-languages-worldwide/
statista.com/statistics/273291/number-of-people-with-malnutrition-worldwide/

United Nations (UN)
un.org/en/sections/issues-depth/population/index.html

UN Children's Fund (UNICEF)/World Health Organization
Progress on household drinking water, sanitation and hygiene 2000–2017
who.int/water_sanitation_health/publications/jmp-report-2019/en/

UN Department of Economic and Social Affairs, Population Dynamics
un.org/development/desa/en/news/population/world-population-prospects-2019.html

UN Educational, Scientific and Cultural Organization (UNESCO)
Institute for Statistics Fact Sheet No. 45 September 2017
uis.unesco.org/sites/default/files/documents/fs45-literacy-rates-continue-rise-generation-to-next-en-2017_0.pdf

Global Education Monitoring (GEM) Report
en.unesco.org/gem-report

unesco.org/new/en/unesco/events/prizes-and-celebrations/celebrations/international-days/international-womens-day-2014/women-ed-facts-and-figure

World Water Development Report 2020
unesdoc.unesco.org/ark:/48223/pf0000372985.locale=en

UN Food and Agriculture Organization (FAO)
fao.org/news/story/en/item/1238015/icode
fao.org/3/ca9692en/online/ca9692en.html#

UN Habitat
unhabitat.org/up-for-slum-dwellers-transforming-a-billion-lives-campaign-unveiled-in-europe

UN International Telecommunication Unit (ITU)
itu.int/en/ITU-D/Statistics/

United States Census Bureau
census.gov/popclock/print.php?component=counter

United States Energy Information Administration
International Energy Outlook, 2019
eia.gov/outlooks/ieo/pdf/ieo2019.pdf

World Bank Group
worldbank.org/en/topic/poverty/overview
data.worldbank.org/indicator/EG.ELC.ACCS.ZS
data.worldbank.org/indicator/SP.POP.TOTL.FE.ZS

World Data Lab
worldhunger.io/

World Economic Forum
weforum.org/agenda/2016/11/which-countries-are-best-at-english-as-a-second-language-4d24c8c8-6cf6-4067-a753-4c82b4bc865b/

World Health Organization (WHO)
who.int
who.int/news/item/21-05-2019-more-people-have-access-to-electricity-than-ever-before-but-world-is-falling-short-of-sustainable-energy-goals
who.int/news/item/15-07-2019-world-hunger-is-still-not-going-down-after-three-years-and-obesity-is-still-growing-un-report

Worldometer
worldometers.info/undernourishment/
worldometers.info/world-population/

Text copyright © 2021 by Egmont Books UK Ltd

Cover art and interior illustrations copyright © 2021 by Aaron Cushley

All rights reserved. Published in the United States by Crown Books for Young Readers, an imprint of Random House Children's Books, a division of Penguin Random House LLC, New York. Originally published by Egmont Books UK Ltd, London, in 2021.

Crown and the colophon are registered trademarks of Penguin Random House LLC.

Visit us on the Web! rhcbooks.com

Educators and librarians, for a variety of teaching tools, visit us at RHTeachersLibrarians.com

Library of Congress Cataloging-in-Publication Data is available upon request.

ISBN 978-0-593-31070-0 (hardcover) — ISBN 978-0-593-37233-3 (ebk)

Written by Jackie McCann
Project Consultant: Mike Goldsmith
MANUFACTURED IN MALAYSIA
10 9 8 7 6 5 4 3
First American Edition

Random House Children's Books supports the First Amendment and celebrates the right to read.

Penguin Random House LLC supports copyright. Copyright fuels creativity, encourages diverse voices, promotes free speech, and creates a vibrant culture. Thank you for buying an authorized edition of this book and for complying with copyright laws by not reproducing, scanning, or distributing any part in any form without permission. You are supporting writers and allowing Penguin Random House to publish books for every reader.

Written by Jackie McCann

Illustrated by Aaron Cushley

IF THE WORLD WERE 100 PEOPLE

A Visual Guide to Our Global Village

CROWN BOOKS
FOR YOUNG READERS
New York

How many people are there in the world?

There are almost 8 billion of us and we're scattered all over the planet! What is life like for everyone? Do you think it's the same? It's tricky to picture 8,000,000,000 people, so instead, let's imagine the whole planet is a village where 100 people live.

Welcome to our global village! Come and meet the people who live here. Each person represents 80 million people (more or less) in the real world. How many children and grown-ups are there? Are there more males or females? Let's find out. . . .

50 people are female

26 people out of 100 are children under 14 years old

50

people are male

8 people out of 100 are more than 65 years old

If we focus on 100 people, it's easier to see the things we have in common and the things that make us different.

How different are we?

Take a good look at your friends—do they look like you or are they different? Everyone on the planet is completely unique. Isn't it amazing! But why is that? Well, we are all made of trillions of cells, each of which contains molecules of DNA. . . .

DNA is in every cell in your body. It has two long strands that are joined together like a twisted ladder. DNA carries all the information that a living thing needs to live and grow. This is called the genetic code and 99.9 percent of your genetic code is exactly the same as everyone else's. It's the tiny 0.1 percent difference that makes you YOU.

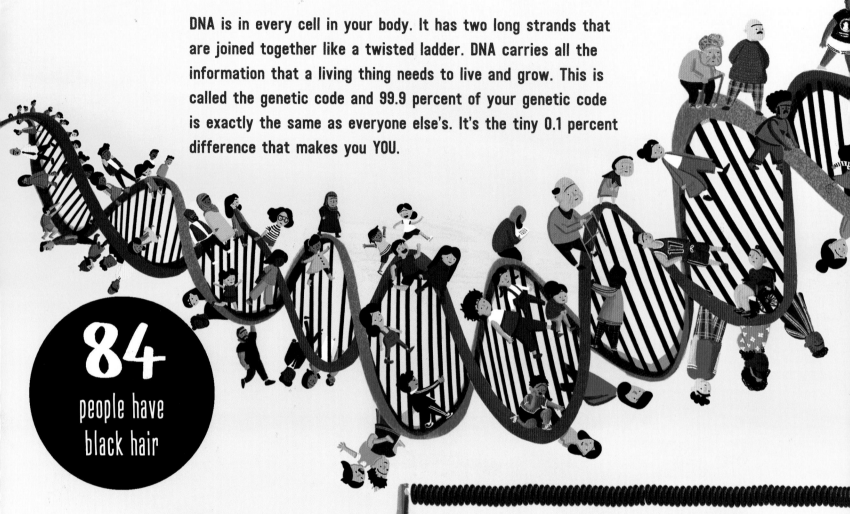

84
people have
black hair

DNA is responsible for your unique fingerprints, hair color, eye color, and lots of other things. Look at this abacus—can you see which eye color is the most common in our village? Which eye-color group do you belong to?

76 people have brown eyes

9 people have blue eyes

5 people have amber eyes

5 people have hazel eyes

3 people have gray eyes

2 people have green eyes

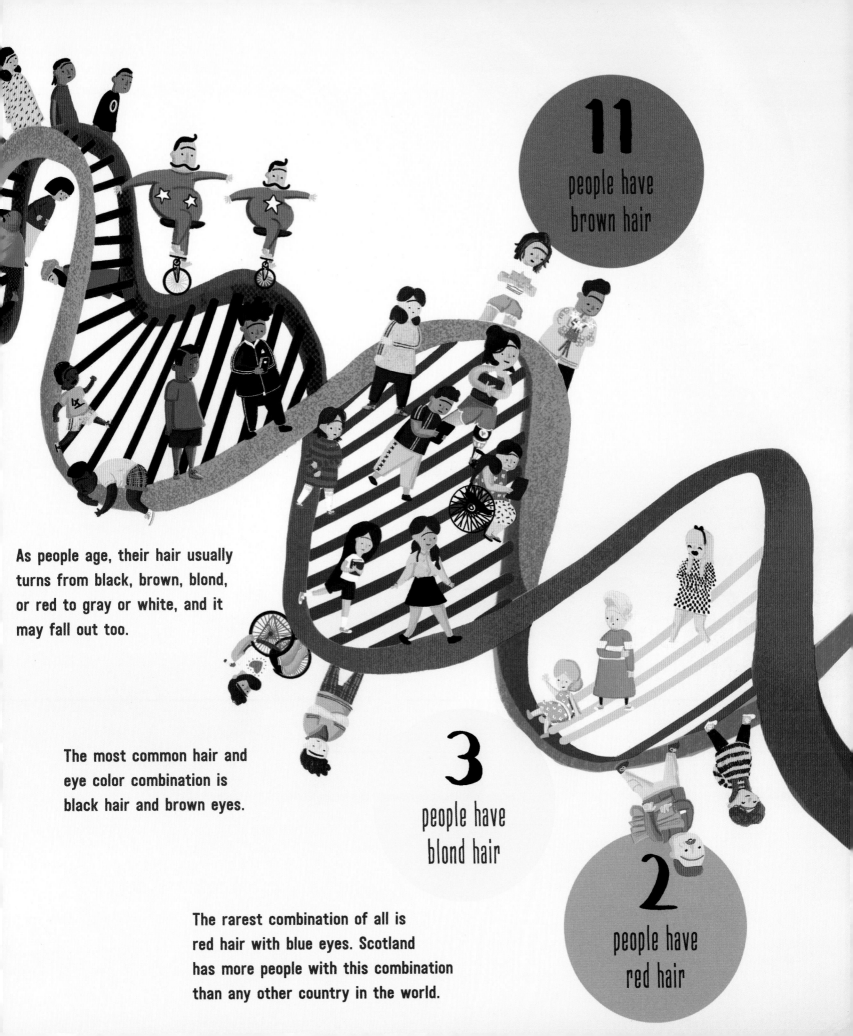

11
people have
brown hair

As people age, their hair usually turns from black, brown, blond, or red to gray or white, and it may fall out too.

The most common hair and eye color combination is black hair and brown eyes.

3
people have
blond hair

The rarest combination of all is red hair with blue eyes. Scotland has more people with this combination than any other country in the world.

2
people have
red hair

5

people live in North America

NORTH AMERICA

Pacific Ocean

Atlantic Ocean

Where does everyone live?

Earth has seven continents, but people only live on six of them. No one lives in Antarctica (except for a small number of scientists). Can you guess why? *Brrrrrr.*

Equator

SOUTH AMERICA

In our global village, people are spread far and wide. Look at the map and you will see that more people live north of the equator than south of it. That's because there is more land in the north. Asia has the fastest-growing population of all the continents—more than half of all the people in the world live there.

8

people live in South America

10 people live in Europe

60 people live in Asia

16 people live in Africa

1 person lives in Oceania

Arctic Ocean

ASIA

EUROPE

Pacific Ocean

AFRICA

Indian Ocean

Equator

OCEANIA

Southern Ocean

ANTARCTICA

Fifty years ago, most people lived in the countryside, but today, most of us live in cities. In the future, most people will live in megacities.

Do you have a place to call home?

Whether you live in a town house, a single family home, a log cabin in the woods, an apartment, a clay hut, or a wooden house on stilts, most people have somewhere to live. But not everyone in our village is so lucky.

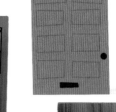

Twenty people in our village do not have a safe home. They may live in cheaply made, unsafe structures that are crammed together. These temporary homes are often knocked down to clear the land. When that happens, people are left homeless.

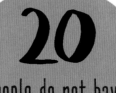

20
people do not have a safe home

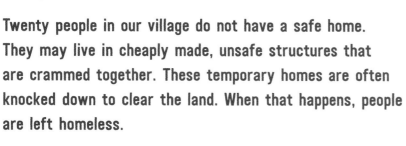

80

people do have
a safe home

How do you say "hello"? *Nǐ hǎo*, *hola*, *namastē*, and *konnichiwa* are just some of the ways that people greet each other. There are around 7,000 languages spoken in the world today, but what do the people in our village speak as their first language?

3 people speak Portuguese

olá

[*say* oh-la]

17 people speak Chinese

nǐ hǎo

[*say* nee-how]

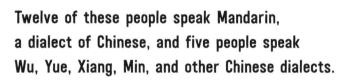

Twelve of these people speak Mandarin, a dialect of Chinese, and five people speak Wu, Yue, Xiang, Min, and other Chinese dialects.

3 people speak Bengali

as-salamu alaikum

[*say* as-salamu-alay-koom]

5 people speak English

Four of them are from North America

English is the most widely spoken second language in the world.

4 people speak Hindi   namastē
[*say* na-mas-tay]

4 people speak Arabic
marhabaan
[*say* mar-har-bahn]

2 people speak Japanese
konnichiwa
[*say* kohn-nee-chee-wah]

6
people speak Spanish
hola
[*say* oh-lah]

2
people speak Russian
privet
[*say* pree-vyet]

54 people speak other languages
as their first language

Can everyone read and write?

The good news is that 86 people over the age of 15 know how to read and write. They get their books from schools and libraries, or are lucky enough to have their own books at home.

Things were very different 200 years ago. Only 12 people over the age of 15 COULD read and write. Today, it's the other way around—14 people in our village over the age of 15 CAN'T read or write. More people go to school now, so our global village is better educated than ever before.

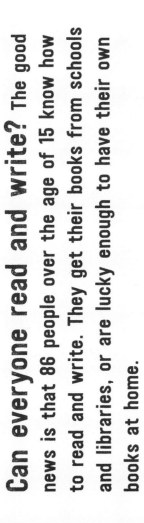

86 people can read or write

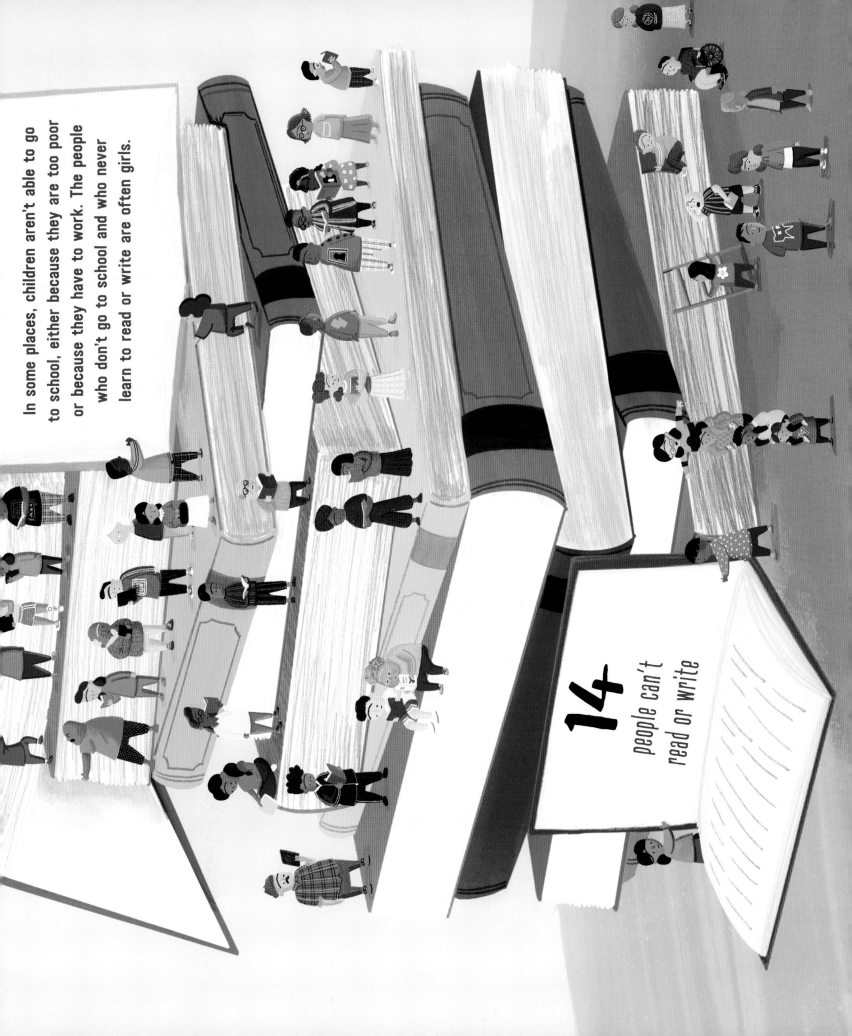

In some places, children aren't able to go to school, either because they are too poor or because they have to work. The people who don't go to school and who never learn to read or write are often girls.

14 people can't read or write

Is there enough food to go around?

We have enough food on the planet to feed everyone,
but it isn't divided equally and not everyone is well fed.
Most people have plenty to eat, but others do not and
sometimes they are very hungry.

89 people have enough to eat

11 people don't have enough to eat

Every year, about a third of all the food produced in the world goes to waste. That is more than enough to feed the 11 people who are hungry.

Do you have clean water at home?

The answer is probably YES! You can drink water, brush your teeth, wash your hands and clothes, and water the garden, simply by turning on a tap. But it isn't the same story for everyone.

71 people have clean water that they can drink or use anytime

In some places, people have to travel a long way to find safe drinking water. Most of the time, it is fetched by women, the elderly, and girls. Sometimes this prevents girls from going to school, which means they may not learn to read and write. This is because in some countries, educating boys is thought to be more important than educating girls.

29

people do not have access to clean water

When people don't have clean water to drink or wash themselves with, they are at risk of catching diseases.

Do you use a computer or watch TV?

What do these activities have in common? Both use electricity! Electricity is a type of energy, and most of the energy we use every day and rely upon comes from fossil fuels. But does everyone have access to it?

90

people have access
to electricity

80% of the energy used by everyone on the planet comes from fossil fuels. Oil, coal, and gas are fossil fuels, and they are formed naturally from the remains of ancient animals and plants.

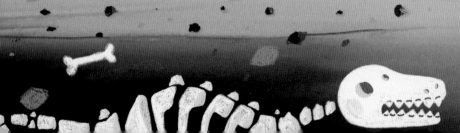

Burning fossil fuels is the biggest cause of greenhouse gases being released into the atmosphere. Greenhouse gases are the main reason why the temperature of the earth is rising and climate change is happening.

We can measure the impact of all our activities on the environment—it's called our carbon footprint. Every time you go to school on the bus or by car, or use electricity to turn on a light you produce carbon dioxide. The weight of the carbon dioxide is your carbon footprint.

10
people do not have access to electricity

11% of the world's power comes from nuclear energy.

9% of the world's energy comes from renewable sources, such as the sun, wind, and water.

Are you connected to the internet?

👍! #! ☺! Do you use a computer at school? Perhaps you have a tablet or smartphone at home? It's hard to believe that the World Wide Web was invented only 30 years ago, as a way of sharing information between computers. Now more than half the world is online!

59 people have internet access

Most people connect to the internet using a smartphone.

#DONTLOOKDOWN

Jeremiah
Tap to view 15s ago

Abdullah
Tap to chat 1m ago

Mariah
Tap to view 10min ago

Jason91
▷ Opened 1h ago ✓✓

Winston_42
◻ received 7min ago

Amelia 🌷🌷
▷ Opened 10s ago

Maya●🌷
▷

Samantha

Nicole

MARLEY HOURLY

♡ ○ ⊳

♥ LOL

👀👀👀

DAVE

#DOGFILTERDAYS

10+

WATER PARK DAYS

By 2030, 90 percent of the world's population will be online, which means that almost everyone in our village will have access to the internet.

⚠ **41** people do not have access to the internet

Is there enough money for everyone?

Yes, there's a lot! Some people also own plenty of real estate, cars, planes, boats, jewelry, and other things of value. Added together with money, it's called wealth. In our village, a few people have almost ALL the wealth in the world. That's because these things aren't shared equally and some people have so much more than others. . . .

10 people have 85% of all the wealth in the world

Almost everyone in our village shares only 15 percent of all the wealth in the world. When we see what people earn in a day, the gap between the people who earn the most and those who earn the least is wide.

50 people live on roughly $7 or more per day. 24 people live on roughly $3.50 to $7 per day. 16 people live on roughly $2 to $3.50 per day. 10 people have less than $2 per day to live on. (These people are very poor and often go hungry.)

90
people have only 15%
of all the wealth
in the world

What are the big questions?

Let's consider what the world will be like in the future. In 2050, there will be about 10 billion people in the world. That's the same as having another Europe and Africa on the planet. What will our global village look like then?

There will be 26 more of us in our village. And there will be many more people over the age of 65 because people are living longer, thanks to better food and medicine. How will we make sure our parents and grandparents are well cared for?

How can we make sure that everyone will have enough to eat in 2050? We already grow enough to feed 10 billion people, but we waste almost a third of all the food we produce. How can we reduce waste and improve the way we share the food we have?

If we waste as much food as we do now, we'll need to produce at least 50% more food.

More people will live in cities than ever before! The good news is that people living in towns and cities generally have better access to clean drinking water, food, hospitals, and medicines. But cities use a huge amount of energy. . . .

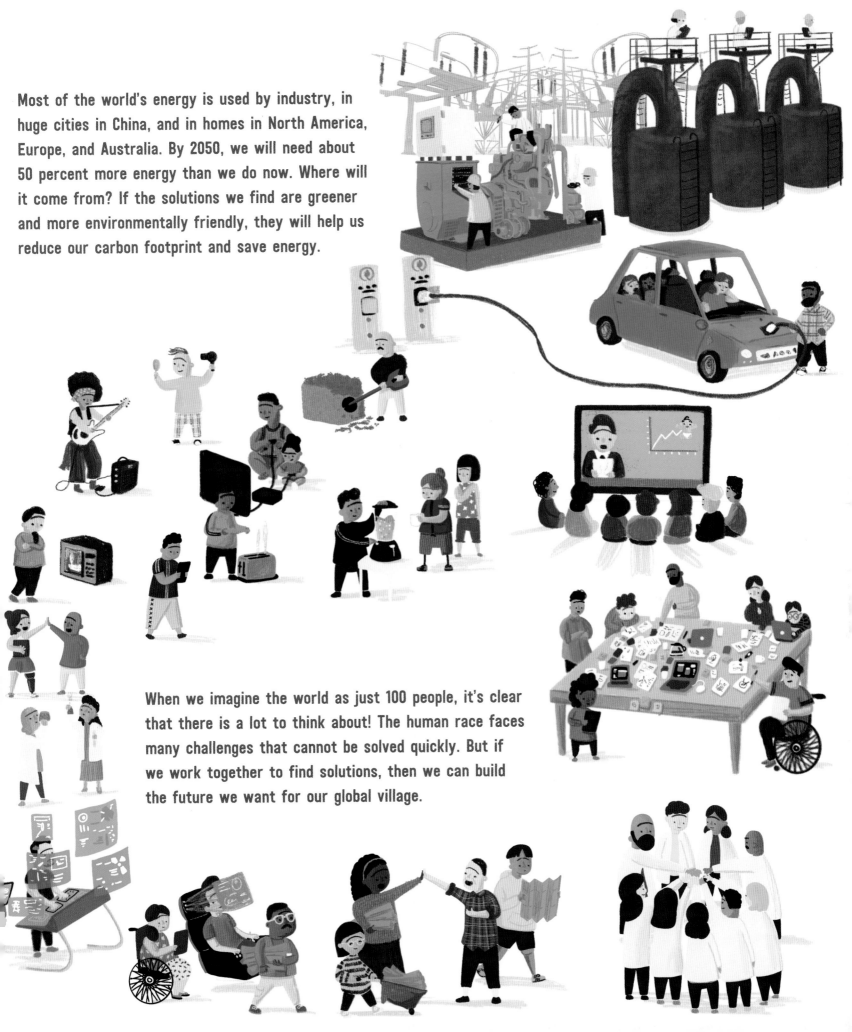

Most of the world's energy is used by industry, in huge cities in China, and in homes in North America, Europe, and Australia. By 2050, we will need about 50 percent more energy than we do now. Where will it come from? If the solutions we find are greener and more environmentally friendly, they will help us reduce our carbon footprint and save energy.

When we imagine the world as just 100 people, it's clear that there is a lot to think about! The human race faces many challenges that cannot be solved quickly. But if we work together to find solutions, then we can build the future we want for our global village.